you

only

love

me

when

i'm

suffering

POEMS

Jon Lupin
the poetry bandit

Castle Point Books
New York

CONTENTS

stillness

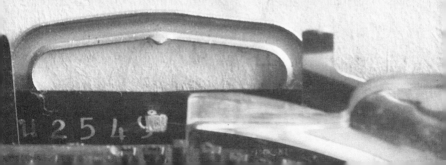

Stillness

When I sit still
I can feel the difficult days
looking at me,
staring hard,
cracking their gnarled knuckles
waiting for another chance
to finish what we started,
but I'll be damned
if I sit still
one second longer
and make it easy
for those bastards.

Wonder

What we all need today is a bit of
    wonder,
Something to take the pragmatic
    realists by the throat
and squeeze, gently, but just hard
    enough
to let them know
that we, the dreamers, mean business.
Enough is enough.
Life has been given the worst of odds,
and I for one,
am tired of rolling dice whenever
    I go out
to work a job that won't matter in
    fifty years.
So, give them a good shark,
write your sweetness down and
cast it in the fire in a mold
that will let your grandchildren know
that once upon a time
we dreamt without fear.

Broad Canvas

We all ask for more,
for a wider canvas to
paint a grandiose picture
of a life dripping in the
brightest of colours,
for a broader sunrise to
enjoy whilst kissing the
supple lips of the new day.
For me,
I want just a little more
ink in this ribbon;
just enough to type
one phrase
which, read while I'm
on my deathbed,
would give me that
wider sun and
broader canvas.

Breed

Hollow eyes breed
shallow lies,
birthing fallow cries
wherein seeds can be planted,
sins are recanted,
mercy represented.
So wise up,
fill your sober cup
and pray for a clean slate.

Eulogy

What will they say when I am gone?
Will they say that I was
easy to love?
Will they say that it was
easy for you to love me
the way you did?
The answer will echo
from beyond the grave
and only those who
truly loved me the way
I loved you
will hear and understand
that I did so
selflessly
and that I died a
happy man.

Innocence

I need a good blanket,
something strong enough
to soak in the tears
meant for whales to swim in,
something strong enough
to hold me together
when my skin begins to fail me.
I need a good blanket,
like the one I had
when my innocence was still intact.

No Man's Land

Caught in the crosshairs
of embattled old souls and young hearts,
burned scrolls,
poisoned words,
and we hid
in our foxhole
until we could write
once more
with that love for language
that used to dance
on the tip of our
fire-licking tongues.

Misconception

You were supposed to be
my brave one,
but you were hesitant to
break me in,
to roll me over
and beat me with
an encouraging word
when all you wanted to do
was leave.
But I realize now,
even the strongest of women
can be scared
once in a little while.

Window Shopping

I have never found much peace
in the loneliness of looking into
    windows,
cupping my hands around the eyes—
hot impatient breath,
cloudy plate glass—
looking in at everyone else's happiness,
all set up for display with too many
    dollar signs.
I'm tired of window shopping
for acceptance
and the price that comes with it.

Trap Doors

I just need to survive myself
because my self-sabotage
is the only trap worth avoiding.
Everything else I will chalk up to
living life on life's terms.

Followers

Follow this fellow long enough
and you will find yourself
asking questions you thought
had been answered in third grade,
but never came without sweat.
So if you do stick around
to discover some of them,
manage your expectations about
this journey.
The simplest test
will command your bones to stretch
and our minds to meld,
if only but to achieve the
most difficult of breaths:
The one taken in a room full of flame
from a beast that would wish us
failure.

Anthem

Every morning
we all have a unique
opportunity
to tell that nagging
little voice,
you know,
the one who sits in
the dark skies behind
our lighted eyes,
that there is no room
for half-assed effort and
delighted comforts
when
we are trying
to turn
whispers
into anthems.

Controller

The only thing I can control
is my typewriter.
I alone can tell it what to say,
and I alone can silence it,
and unlike a person,
it is always encouraging me
to use it,
abuse it,
control it.
All because it truly wants me
to feel better.

Crowns

Wear your vulnerability
like a crown;
whether it is made
of thorns or
of wildflowers
is up to you.

Angel's Work

I sit here often,
wondering what it is that makes
the heart beat for the first time,
and also what makes it
beat its last.
It is a quiet little thing
compared to the rest of the body.
If only that heart
could beat a little
louder for all humanity
to hear
maybe
angel's work would be done
and this world
would cease to burn alive.

Playmate

When your demons
come to the door
and ask you outside,
play hardball
with your soul.
It's the only one
you have.

Chasm

The space between
your past mistakes
and your future fullness
dwindles and closes
when your eyes
or fixed upon
something greater
than yourself.

Rembrandt

Time painted us a picture
that stood still when we moved,
trying to see if it followed us
when we moved to and fro,
violently or slowly.
Taken with it,
we made off in the
heat of the night,
stashing it in a safe place,
where he would not find it.

Hero

You could never venture out
to the city,
never take a subway late at night,
never walk the darkest alley,
never even call my name
if you needed saving,
but I will never sleep
until I know
your heart
is safe
and all your tears
are ones
of joy.

Live-Model Canvas

There is art
in the gentle slope
of your shoulders,
and a soft soundness
in the dip of
your chin
as you lean in to kiss me
and set all my
colors
free.

Time to Die

"Where does Father Time go
when he has finished with us,
my darling?"
Tender questions from
my lover always give way
to dramatic silences
and something from my mind
like:
"No one knows, but me,
because I was the one
who put a bullet in his skull
and buried him in your
father's field.
I wanted eternity with you."

You Will Never Know

She was gentle with my soul,
cradling my soul
like a flightless, tiny bird,
for that is how she found me.
Injured.
Listless.
Lamenting at how life had
sent me into a tailspin
of self-doubt.
Was I ever meant to fly?
She was kind enough
to answer me,
and what she said
is much too
precious to share.

History

Remember when my stolen flowers
laid upon the crest of your temple,
so gentle as the cool wind of the Bay
kissed your cheeks
as I once had?

When people ask, "What is magic?"
I often think of this moment.

Birdies

We were never singing
the same song,
we were never in tune,
and we were never
in beat,
but that didn't matter
because
we were lovebirds,
not songbirds.

Hike for Life

I like to stand
at the cliff's edge
and play with the
strong winds
that tempt;
beat my eyelids
at the eagles,
try to bring them closer;
beckon the clouds
to come and touch
my face with
gentle persuasion.

I am never afraid
because I am tied
to you,
knotted
forever
in your frame.

Sojourner

She was the one
who taught me how
to pack a suitcase.
With concrete kisses
and warm wet shoes,
I never could tell
if I was supposed to stay
or take the next train
out of town.

A Nice Flat Stone

Thinking I could walk on water
I stepped out of my skin
and tried to take hold
of what I felt was mine,
but slowly each moment
passed
reminding me
I am nothing but
a stone skipped
across the vastness
of the ocean,
careening into eternity,
with nothing tangible
to hold on to.
So
I
let
go
and
let
it
skip
me
to
the
end.

The Other Side

Remove me from my home
and cast my feet in clay,
bring me to the river's edge,
play a song,
make a daisy chain,
dance a dirge,
but all the while
remember
we were born to die,
return to dust,
prey on rust,
with a soul corroding.
But breath
from the other side
will give
new life.

Let it Be

I have a terrible habit
of making a great thought
something that would have been
happier
if I had just
left it
alone.

Bedtime

You begged me for a lullaby,
but I couldn't bring myself
to sing you away
from me again.
For even in rest
that beautiful distance
is too much for me
to endure.

Morning After

My breath is hard
and wasted,
but your sighs
are soft,
so tonight
I will rest
upon your air
and trust
the morning
will be lighter
for me.

Natural

Sweetness flutters
in a strong wind
and I pray she settles
in the long grass
behind my home
so I may show her
where the calm is
after the storm.

Rush Hour

The fingertips of patience
press hard against my lips
when I all want to do is
scream how much I want
to be the one
who you run to.

But I should know better.
You and love
are never in a hurry.

Finality

When I picture my happy day,
the final day of my life,
I see an ocean.
I feel a slight breeze
in a perfect temperature.
I counter the pressure of
your hand in my hand,
squeezing it just hard enough
to feel the bones in your hand
to know this is real.
I see a small cottage,
a soft bed to share,
and have the realization
I had passed on
a while ago
and this was my heaven.

Quest

We are all searching
for what will make us
live forever
in that person's eyes
who matters more
than life itself.
Some of us will find it,
others will not,
and everyone will still
be crazy
at the end.

dirge

You Only Love Me When
I'm Suffering

I can see it is a lonely world
out there.
This is why I am afraid
to let go of you.
I'm afraid that this freefall
will never end,
and you should know
that this is a suffering
in its own right.
And on top of that
to be told
I must
have freedom from you,
to let go
and be my own person.

But,
when you suffer
like I do
from a mental distress
that seems like a
wrinkle in a pair of dress pants
that won't iron out,
no matter how hot the iron is,
then you have no choice
but to want,
to need,
some kind of anchor.

You see,
I need you
more than you
can understand,
right now,
and that is why
I'm afraid
you only
love me
when I'm
suffering.

Spring

He came to cut me up
into tiny pieces
to feed them to
all the little birds
that perch outside
your window
in spring.

Sadness Condensed Upon a Bathroom Mirror

Quietly,
she filled the bathtub
with warm lavender water
and bitter tears,
not caring for what
spilled upon the bathroom floor.

Traveler

You were not from here,
a traveler, like me,
but not exactly like me.
It was clear the first time
my eyes caught your rays
for I had not witnessed colors this
    bright,
this foreign. They were anything
but real.
I was taken
by your golden hues,
intense blues,
mixing in the soft dark light
I was casting
trying to see if you would,
if you could be mine,
to live in this place,
with me and mine.

Maybe that was a dream,
the kind of reverie where dark skin and
silver lips shone through the
sadness we both felt,
knowing this would never last,
that an end was drawing near.
And it did end.
Quickly.
Terribly.
Suddenly.
Today,
I wear these colors often
in the hope that you might glance them
from your side of this life, that side
you will not let me see.

Black Dresses

It will rain on that day,
and it will do so continuously,
bleeding into the saline sadness
dripping from cheek to chin,
from chin to folded hands
in earnest prayer,
asking me to rise from
oak and cushion,
but I will not,
for I will be too busy
looking upon her with ghostly eyes,
settling on her slender form
wrapped gently in a
black little number
I bought for her last month.

Warning Label

Warnings about her,
I never heeded.
I was reckless and aloof,
took her to places where we both lost
our imaginations, specters in the
mist of expectation,
former shells of ourselves,
emptied.
I paid the ultimate price
in heartbreak and sense,
and the world watched,
hands in the air,
sackcloth and ash,
because I would never be
innocent again.

Out of Nothing

I've got nothing.
I wake up most days,
ready with bold teeth barred,
snarling, claws out,
wishing for the baddest beast in town
to just try and burst into my life and
pour some thick porter down my throat
and cast my life into the furnace.
It only takes one word, a tone, one
    second,
one thought, one look at hell
to de-claw me
and make me feel as if the day
was better off without my madness.

But I'm up now,
so I will do my best
to make something
out of nothing.

Furnaces

Tonight,
I burned my hand
while stoking the fire
burning in the furnace
of our collective heart,
and I'm wondering,
is this a sign
of things to come
or was I just a little bit
careless?
Maybe it's a bit of both.

Caesar Salad

There is no difference
between a sharp edge
or a dull one...
if it's in the hands of a friend,
the damage to your
spine
is all the same.

Drama King

When the sirens sound
and my broken heart is
carried away
across borders and through
secret cemeteries,
cast your shadow
in my stead
to rule my world
now that I'm dead.

Hades

My soul hangs from above,
swaying gently in a
breeze from the mouth
of Hades;
heaven hath sent me flowers,
but hell hath sent for me.

Dancing

Deadwood dances in the froth
of a sea that lost its love
for me too early,
and I can't help but
dream about being
tossed about again and again,
terrified and unceasingly,
in a happy anger,
like the way you did
with my
second chances.

Second Hand

When I was built
they must have used
second-hand parts
because I swear
I've felt like this before,
and the second time around
isn't any easier.

Humpty Dumpty

Broken like eggshells
with no army to save me,
I am a slave to the tale
and chained to a wall
from which there is no escape

Code Breaker

Cryptic,
cold and
cynical,
all this before morning,
mourning the face, we slept,
wept and kept the tears
from laying us
sweetly down,
so we stayed up
and drank away
night next,
netting us a
zero return on
being together.

Thaw

You left me out on the counter
to thaw
amongst the carrion
left for the
vultures with
voluptuous appetite
to devour over
a spirit poured
from a dirty earthen vessel,
and when I came to
my bones were strewn
about your living room,
and I floated away
to join the moon.

Gossip

Nothing could be worse
than discourses
while flogging dead horses,
hoarse with no
recourse
than to dice long tongues
for a stew
not even the
homeless would eat.

Bandaged

Twisted in up in my rain-soaked Sunday
     best
I picked last night's feast of fractured
     love from my canines,
panting with panic,
grasping for some semblance of how
to correct this self-vision,
this double-minded daring to ask you
for yet another do-over.
It reeks of last ditch efforts
and broken wings
dressed and bandaged
with busted prayers.

But now,
it's all I know.
And that's ok,
for now.

Tongues

Pretty words
like hummingbirds
flutter and shudder,
starve and waste away
when your tongue
serves poison
instead of nectar.

Lord's Day

I feel most broken
on a Sunday,
when I'm reminded
another week begins
without you.

Catacomb Lovers

If I fail to show you
blood, sinew and tissue,
all which beats inside,
then
turn me to stone
and place my weight
in that catacomb
you keep empty
for people like me
and my broken promises.

White Cedars

It is scientifically proven
that the slowest-growing
tree in the world is
the white cedar,
growing only four inches
every 155 years.
And yet,
time seems to move
slower than this
when you are not here.

Christmas

Something wraps you up
like a Christmas present
bought with care,
meant to seal the deal,
and all you want to do is
rip yourself away from it all
and run naked through the trees,
bare skin decorating in the moonlight,
wild yet contained
to the conditions life has placed on you
when you drew your
first blood,
when you took your first flower,
when you gave it all
to a fantasy that someone out there
would visit and never reveal themselves
and all you got was a sock
meant to be worn
instead of hung out to dry.
This is how it felt when you left.

Bleached

Voices fade in and out
of my memory.
Some scream.
Some lament.
Some whisper,
but yours...
yours sings that sad song
of love gone awry,
of love like a bleached bone
on the rocky shore of a lake
the locals got bored with,
a lake where voices echo,
come and go,
but in that same sad octave
of yours,
which will haunt me forever.

After the Fire

I was ready to set my life on fire
for you.
I was ready to bathe myself
in the ashes of the pictures
I took while loving others.
I was ready to do anything
to clean house and begin anew;
the problem was
by the time I was prepared
to start the work,
you had already gone
and done that on your own.

Christmas in July

Moving on,
but stuck in reverse,
or between the ears,
gumming up the gears,
running through the years
wondering how I ended
my story on sour notes
on more than one occasion
by gnashing my teeth,
crying for one more chance
hoping you won't let me go
like a Christmas tree
still lit and living in July.

Vagabondage

I haven't eaten in quite some time,
and I haven't loved this life
with the zeal it demands.
Don't get me wrong.
I want to be here.
I do.
It's just that
I have this feeling that I am
just passing through, you know?
Like a vagabond in a small town,
or the ghost living in the walls
of your childhood home,
subtle yet deliberate.
I am here,
but not everywhere,
just in the places that you look
for some passing truth.
So while I am supposed
to keep on keeping on,
I will stick around,
just for a little while longer
for I can see you're in the
need for a ghost
but one made of
flesh and bone.

Car Crash

The day dreams often pull me
from my body,
much like a car crash rips a family
into shreds,
and I'm torn between staying
in suspended reality,
a place where my ego allows me
to run the show,
or to collapse back into a ruinous
wreck of a life where I am
always picking up
the pieces of my
busted headlights and
scattering sand
on the cruel mix of
blood and fuel.

Empires

When I look upon the
works of these hands
and all they have wrought,
I cannot help but
wonder why they tremble
when I am without you;
I have built an empire
but without your love
it is but a word
written in the water.

Making

Making you love me
is akin to writing
on crumpled paper,
paper destined for the
flames of a man's doing,
not fit to read or
color with vagrant hues,
and not even pale enough to
bear your praises.
So, here I sit,
with a medium as coarse
as my soul
and a desire empty
of everything but
the ink to spell out
your name upon my skin.

Hologram

Our love was like
a hologram
for without light,
we were nothing.

Love Talks

If Love could talk
She wouldn't.
She knows there are
no words to explain
what happened.
No, instead she would
just hold me,
stroke my cheek,
tenderly,
and tell me the awful,
awful truth
that at one point,
I just wasn't enough.

Ambulatory Care

Doubts pile up
much like the body bags
and John Doe toe tags
on a festival night,
or in the worst of my nightmares.
You know, the ones where
it's just you and me,
but mostly me,
staring at the pink slip
you handed me,
ending a friendship
that was going anywhere
but south,
or so I thought.
And now,
I very much feel
like a flock of birds
searching for their paradise
they know is close but
remains hidden from them
until the cold is here.

Too late for a chance
at a life that
could have been
so much more than the
cold winter's breath,
or your shoulder.
What do I do
when it feels like I'm on
my way to nowhere,
on my way to just
being another person
bagged and tagged,
ignored and forgotten,
waiting with all the
body bags,
having missed their chances
at a life full of warmth?

Hangman

I don't wear a tie
when I dress up
to dine with you
anymore;
there's enough in
our world
trying to choke me out
and I don't need a
piece of linen
to finish the job.

All of the Things

Hurt, laughter,
joy, sadness,
anger, confusion.
All these I make room for
on my sleeve
right next to my heart.
That is where it sits
Because I believe
it likes the view of
you a little too much.
And it gets lonely there
for my heart.
The other feelings
push it around,
bully it in a passive aggressive way
that makes high school
seem like a cake walk.
But it refuses to move,
it refuses to tear its gaze
from where you are.
So that's where it stays,
for now,
at least until you
decide on whether
you're going to join in
with the bullies
or rescue it.

Survival

Weak sheep
or
bold wolf;
at one point
in our lives
we will be
both
in order
to survive
what's to come.

Cherubim

We speak the truths
you cannot cover
with candy or with a
choir of angels,
though each one sings
at the top of their
airy lungs.
And that is why
we get treated like devils,
burned under
hot, dried gazes
at stakes dressed up
in ribbons and bows;
the world will always
fear us
and the
fun we bring along.

Papercut

Tonight,
we will bleed out
an honesty that will
bring about a change
in the hearts of all
men and women.
It will bring hope to
children who will
never have to bleed out
for any cause,
any one person,
any belief,
or any one colour.

This is what
the blood
of the honest souls
should bring about
in the hearts
of a
complacent
nation
when it spills
upon the
battlefield
of life.

Raynaud's Syndrome

I have this thing where
the nerves in my feet and hands
pinch off my blood vessels,
draining the life from them,
turning them plain white,
like an albino android.
Lately,
it happens more and more often,
as if my body is preparing me
for the days when the warmth
of your sun will be hidden from me
and I will need to get
used to the feeling
of not being able to
hold on to anything
or stand firm.

Enabler

I will no longer prey upon
your desire to drink in the
quick fix to all your fears;
from now on you will only
hear what you think you
cannot handle:
there is a world
that does not come home
for dinner,
it's out there playing with
all the cool kids,
trying to bury them early,
with all the tricks of a
seasoned salesman,
and if you're not careful
it will be me
who will be worried sick
when your seat
at the supper table
isn't filled.

Artist in the Making

Many times painted
with the same brush,
with the same colors,
which today,
just don't seem bright enough
to hide how I truly feel.
So,
if I'm going to sit here
and let you tell me
how to paint
a perfect version of my life,
I will need to be the one
who picks the colors,
shades the hues,
strikes the pose
because I want you
to know
that when this work of art
is done
I will hang it
next to the mirror
you smashed,
over the holes you left
in the walls
and in my heart
and I will be proud
of what I see.

It's Lit

A million matches lit,
trying to ignite one
simple flame
between you and me.
It turned into a
firestorm
and burnt me
to the ground.

Carrion

Truth circles
like vultures
waiting to feast
upon
my dying wish:
that you had
never left.

Trauma

I bleed as if there is no bandage
that could keep me
from splitting all the way open,
that could keep my feelings
from spilling
ruthlessly
upon the freshly cut grass.
So alas,
thine damage is done
and I am forever
your *Amen*,
but at least you
let me mow the lawn
first.

WMDs

You invaded my heart
looking for love,
for what it meant to be
the subject of my desire,
but all you found
was a weapon
of mass destruction.

Taste Test

You asked me
what heartache
tasted like,
so I told you
to bite your
tongue
and let me know.

151 Proof

I am a fickle misfit
fighting fretting fathers
only for a chance
to prove to them
I belong here,
knee-deep in
liquor and
manic lucidity
as much as the
next bastard.

Hansel

Be careful of which
path you choose
when searching
for sweetness,
or you might
find yourself
licking the knives
of crazy old wives.

A Tiny Piece of Wood

Like a splinter
you inserted
a tiny word
under my skin,
into my veins,
and it made me
crawl
right
back
into
you.

Clinical

You and I,
we were like that
synapse in the mind,
constantly misfiring
and causing
catastrophe
in the clinic.

We were a
public
display
of infection
and no one
was safe
from us.

Eve

She picked hearts
like she would choose
forbidden fruit,
a supple and
delicious rebellion.

Days of Yore

I was a story
rolled in fine glory,
drenched in the desire
for more,
and bleeding
from the core,
still,
always
wanting
more.

Flogged

I will bare my back
and have it switched
until the streets run red
with my blood
if only for another chance
at life,
free of the brambles,
shame
and
fables.

Cemetery Love

We jumped tombstones
at night
and ran naked through
the cemetery
hoping Death wouldn't
see our souls
for what they were:
dying to be in love
with each other.

Catch-22

A sip of coffee,
and I will light this world on fire.

A sip of whiskey,
and I will burn along with it.

Dirge

When the fading sunset
dances its last ballet
across my face,
it will be followed by a
dirge of the drowning sorrow
I feel when I think of
all those friendly faces
I miss the most when
I'm lost in an ocean of
my own making.

emptiness

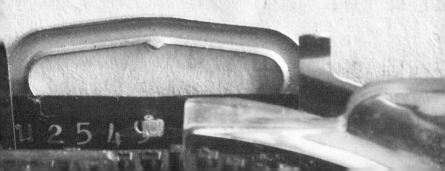

Empty, Like a Church in Montreal

We hung like a chandelier
in an empty church;
derelict and damned
we were cursed to have
our light burn
for no one.

Chaff

My will was scattered
like chaff left to be blown away
by a gust of wind
to the four corners
of this planet.
It burned softly
with the sins of
my youth.

The Show

If you're going to let me burn,
the least you could do
is stick around
and watch the show.

In the Ring

The gloves came off
long before
I learned how to
tape and lace,
because the fight
I will not lose
is right between
my ears.
Even though
I may bruise
on the outside,
beneath this
battle skin
beats the heart
of a lion,
and those feelings that
stand in my way
are my prey.

Road Trip

Now I know what prison feels like,
stuck here in my hotel room
like a caged animal,
foaming at the mouth,
fangs sharpened with nothing
to carve but a shiv
out of this desk
that is shoved into the corner
of the room,
with one working light
to shine in interrogation on being
steps away from what I want
but miles away from what I need.
Cravings.
They bring me to a state of
animalism,
imprisoned and
impoverished of the
ability to speak to others,
to have a conversation,
sit amongst other people.
Because,
if I see them drinking
I'll be convicted by
my cravings and I'll be
steps away from what I need
but miles away from what I really want:
happiness.

Pied Piper

You were the
Pied Piper
of the petty and
the pretty,
preying on their
fears that one day
they might fade away
and have nothing left
to stare at during the
long hours of the night
when the soul
dies just a little bit
with each and every
selfish thought.

Rumpelstiltskin

On nights like this
I leave you behind,
choking on my words
spun from gold I stole
from a greedy little man
while he was having a
nightmare,
because no one has lived
this life like I have
and I'm not about to let
you tell me
how to be
valuable again.

Honest Cup of Coffee

Honesty buys us nothing these days.
Maybe it will buy me a cup of coffee,
burnt with forgetfulness in a mug
    that looks
white but has been stained with years
    of pours
and years of being gripped by a nation
afraid to finish it,
to pay and enter a world where everyone
and everything has abandoned truth
for that easier, softer way.
A way rife with one-liners sprayed
    with paint
and carelessness.
It makes me sick to my stomach,
makes me raise hell like a man raises
    his children
but I'm really just left with nothing
    to say,
because nothing
changes
anyway.

So, just let me drink this
cheap cup of joe and pretend
there's nothing afterwards to do
but smile.

Fool

Hot tea
and
cold feet;
I am just
another
lonely foot
waiting around
in a coffee shop
for a
girl like you.

Cruelty

Zipper up
and pull your thin skin
tighter
around those frailties
and await the
cruel storm of works
from a ruthless world,
but know,
if you just ask,
there is a blanket
thick enough to
cover you in the
memories you once loved,
once upon a time,
in a lover now
very far away.
I can bring it closer,
if you let me.

Worry

My body pulses with the
heavy dead-weighted beat of my heart.
This doesn't feel
very much like living to me.
It pounds because there is no longer
any blood to spare.
Worry courses through my veins
and fills each chamber
like a badly kept secret
at a dinner party
where everyone is playing
a game of Russian roulette.

Learning to let go
is hard
when the gun
is myself.

Squeeze

You wanted me
to love you
like the
elements love each other,
but you should know,
you can't get
sunlight
when you squeeze a rock.

Cold Java

The coffee always went cold
before I had a chance to tell
her how much I needed her to stay.
I blame myself for the
stagnancy and the status quo,
and try to be at peace with
cold shoulders
and lukewarm love.

Alcoholic

I had a heart once.
It did all the things
all the other hearts do,
like pump out great ideas,
dance to its own beat,
clean up the blood from
the noses of friends who
wanted to just see me succeed.

But it unraveled
somewhere between
the first drink
and the last.

Three-Word Stories

You love those little sayings,
don't you?
You hold them close,
put them in special places
hoping to read them
and have your hair
stand up on end
and a little dramatic tear
careen down those perfect cheeks.
But we both know,
that doesn't really happen.
If it did work,
the three-word story
I wrote about us
should have been enough.

Born Again

We are all
born with big hearts;
some of us,
unfortunately,
choose not to
ever grow into theirs.

Silent Repeater

For me,
repetition is the act
of compulsion and
compulsion the act
of desiring security
and control.
And the feeling of security
is bred out of the lack
of having
someone
to kiss
goodnight.

Lonely Insomniac

It doesn't matter
if I lie in bed
on my side,
on my back,
or on my chest.
It's always in
darkness
without
you
breathing
next
to
me.

Apologies

I am sorry,
I am sorry I am different now.
I'm sorry that I was drinking
while they tended to you
and wrote songs,
songs I once sang.
I am sorry I cannot drink
like all your friends can,
and I am sorry
I am a shell of the
confident man
I used to be.

But.

I am working on it,
and even though
you do not know
how to help me,
your touch,
your love,
your trust in
knowing I will make
progress
is all I want.

I am sorry,
and one day
I won't be
apologizing
anymore.

Princess

It was said that she never
took a bad photo
and never looked
worse for wear,
but underneath
all that praise and
expensive eyeliner
was a pretty little girl
who wanted to live her life
in the last chapter of
her fairy tale
and not be stuck in the first.

Scotch and Ease

Raw and ethereal,
slippery like a ghost
is that fleeting feeling felt,
skin scrawling
a rescue note
in sweat on my floor.
And when no one came,
I slithered out from
underneath my bed
and stepped out
into the light.
I tried to run from it,
but like some scared
little sheep
that feeling of inadequacy
always followed me
like wine and cheese,
scotch with ease
and just like that
I was right back
to being underneath.

Tissues

Today she feels like
the tissue box
I just emptied into
my eyes.

Today was just a bad day,
and tomorrow,
another chance for me
to show her
why I stay.

Lost

Every tear is a
salty reminder
of the softest things
in life lost,
and I
do not want
you
to become
one of them.

Hypochondriac

There are diseases of the body
of the soul,
of the mind,
and will keep you alive
while they eat away
at your resolve,
but I have an ailment
of the heart,
and without you
I fear my days
are numbered.

The Sum

Over the past few years
I have lost parts of myself
that made me
who I am.
The sum of those
missing pieces
total a cost
I had not expected,
and now,
I feel as if I should go
looking for them
to see if they banded
together
and
created a better life
than the one I had
destroyed.

Dungeon Dweller

I like to sit in my basement
barefoot,
the cold of the concrete floor
seeps into my bones
and reminds me
that I am living life
one foot in the ground
and I shouldn't spend it
in the cold and dank places
for too long.

Side Effects

There is a smoothing over
of my personality
happening,
as we speak.
Forces unknown,
sobriety,
how I perceive
how you want me to be,
a small yellowish-orange pill
roughly 5mg in dosage,
it's all taking away
the parts of me
that made me
who I am,
who I was
when you met me.

Maybe that is why
this is harder than
I had anticipated.
If I'm no longer
the man I was
when you met me,
will you cease to
love me
for who I am?

I'm changing,
differing,
buffering,
and while everyone else
is breathing a
sigh of relief,
I'm just over here
just trying to sigh
without yawning
myself into
zombie land.

Crowd Surfing

We passed through
the murder of crowds,
but longed for the
quiet faces to step out
and pull us from
the pecking order,
just to tell us
what a smile looked
like again and
simply cared that
we were alive
and not hanging
on a post in some
abandoned field
of corn.

Color Wheel

The absence of love
has the same color
my shadow has,
and it doesn't seem to
matter how I dress
him up,
my shadow will
always feel a little
down in the doldrums
without you
around
to shine a light.

Frozen Shoulders

It is cold,
the unknown.
I shiver
knowing
without you here,
I will lose
my heart
to frostbite.
Twice shy
to realization
that there isn't anything
I can do about it.
I am told to
move on,
carry on,
all the clichés ending
with "on,"
and nothing is
more frustrating
for me.
I just can't do it.
I can't.
If you're shoulder
isn't a balmy
98 degrees
then I'm afraid
I'm staying put
until the weather
turns around
for me.

The Good Kind

Side by side,
tooth in nail,
blood and vein,
no wind, all sail,
and if I had
one breath left
I would send it
to you in the mail,
but I am anchored
to my floor
and longing for that
good kind of grief
again.

Circles

The circles
under her eyes
seemed just
dark enough
for me to
hide my sins
there.

flicker

Flicker

There was a flicker
in your eyes
so divine
it reminded me
that mine were
built for more
than just crying.

Growth

And though I might be
just another weed in this
overgrown garden hall,
leave me
and I will show you
how beautiful I can be.

Homebody.
I could have gone out
and lit any candle I wanted,
but I chose to stay here
and stoke your fire,
burning in angelic light.

Clear

In a single moment
of clarity
I knew you only ever
had to say,
"I love you" once,
and that it should be
enough for me,
forever.

Hospitable

Come in,
sit down and warm yourself
at the hearth of my love;
stay a while
and tell me your woe,
tell me what creased your
precious face
at such a young age.
Spare no detail,
spare me no mercy,
and pour your fragility
out upon the floor
and let me mop it up.

Let's get you out of that
sadness
and into something
more comfortable,
shall we?

Maelstrom

Our love was a
maelstrom;
we never stood still
long enough
for reality
to tear us apart.

Kaleidoscope

I held you up
to the sun
and looked through you
like a kaleidoscope
and saw all the things
I wanted to see.

Three Little Birds

I have three little birds
that house themselves,
built a nest of sorts
inside my heart.
They come and perch
perfectly still,
patiently paused
waiting for me
to tell you their names,
those three little names
you longed to hear
flutter from my lips.

Mad

There isn't much these days
to stir my soul
the same way your touch can,
and I guess this is why
I put one thought in front
of the next,
block out the dark ones
and embrace the lighter ones.
Because when you live
in the midst of obsession,
you are the only thought
worth going over;
if this isn't a testament to
how much you drive me crazy
I don't know what else to say
but,
let me go mad,
and let your hug be my
straight jacket
and your kiss
that saline shot in my arm.

Theme Song

When you walk the other way
I always feel like
the music in my head
becomes very dramatic
and in a key and tempo
that lets me know
you'll be back
one day.

Chapter 11

She made it clear to me
she wouldn't be bought
with riches
so I sold my soul
and followed her,
bankrupt
but happy.

Victory

You took me away
from home
and gave me wings,
unfurled like the
flag of the victor,
and I was begotten
to the wind,
seeking a new place
to hang my coat
and hat.

The B-Side

Rant on with wanton,
never pleased,
ravaged with ease,
no longer kind,
I forgot to rewind,
so take me back
to the days
when it was okay
to blow kisses
at strangers
on this crazy side
of heaven.

Excited

I get cold when I get excited,
and the only way I can explain
    that is by
figuring I'm looking forward
subconsciously for the end,
an eternal cold,
where skin, bone and ghost part ways,
that final tea party
where discussion is on happier times,
harmonious memories
and the love felt for a gift
we were happy wasn't wasted
on a life lived in the gutter.

Vapor

Love's song
is but a vapor,
skipping across
the waters of our souls,
waiting to be ignited
and set our lives
on fire
in a flame we
can be proud of.

Forester

A forest,
deep and glum,
breaking branches
whilst walking freely
not caring for the crunch
and crackling kindling
we could have gathered.
We took the dark as a friend
and the light as a foe,
made trails
and forgot to mark the way
the way back home.
We were unprepared,
and even though
we knew we'd be lost
for a time,
we were foresters
frolicking in fear
trying something new.

Dreamers

What was it about tomorrow
that brought us back
to this idea of
making love our
endless dream?
Time after time,
fight after fight,
awkward silence after
awkward moment?
I guess it was always about
knowing everything was going
to be just fine,
because we knew
in our hearts
we were dreamers,
in love with each other
and each other's fantasies.

Today

Today has had its way
with you, but fear not,
its grip will loosen,
its gaze will soften,
its words will mean a little less
as night falls about you
like the blanket your
grandmother used to
tuck you in with.
Tomorrow is nearly here,
and along with it,
so many more reasons to
put down the
foolish notion
that this world would
never miss you;
I would miss you.
I would miss us.

China Doll

Tip-toeing through rooms
of sleeping giants,
we hope to escape a
life rife with
boredom.
We wanted to be free
to drink our coffee
under the stars
instead of in homes
decked out in delft blue
and porcelain dolls
with empty eyes,
for we were afraid
of becoming like them,
pure white
with no life.

Fairy Tales

She never knew why I stayed,
despite the eye socket torrents,
the false hope and faded starts,
I felt that
it was never about living life perfectly
or about loving someone without fault.
It was never about the actual story,
the chapters we could write,
the gripping prologue
or an epilogue dripping in melancholy,
or even about the storybook ending
that seemed so inevitable to you.
What she failed to see
was that, to me, it was all about her;
her flesh on mine,
her lips firmly locked in a caress
that would set
every storybook villain on fire
and turn every book to ash.
Everything else would fall into place
as long as my place
was always right beside her,
no matter what peril we faced.

Speechless

I must have stared at this page for
    about only a minute
before I knew what I wanted to say
    to you,
and now that I have it set out,
word for word,
hand gestures all planned,
prepared to maintain eye contact
with you during the soft and
    sweet parts,
all the while trembling with excitement
on how you will receive this masterpiece
in the many rooms of your giant heart,
I cannot say a bloody word.
I cannot,
for you have captured
each and every breath
with that simple smile,
with the sway of your hips,
with that gentle touch on my forearm
as you walk by...
and I am okay with this.
For even though I have lost my oration
I saved three little words
for just such an occasion.

Singularity

I remember the first time we kissed
for it was the first time
I had been shown
what love was capable of,
and because I had tasted it
on the crest of your mouth
and on the tip of your tongue,
my rebellion towards a
life lived in singularity
was quieted and laid to rest.

Tremble

The treble in your
trembling is
troublesome,
but hang on,
deep breaths,
listen for me
in the low notes
of your life
because that is
where I hide,
and there is
plenty of room
for you here
to join me.

Dead Shakespeare

There is no longer anything
to compare this love to.
So ends all the poems,
all the musings,
all the sonnets and similes,
metaphors and meteoric phrases.
The page rests and
breathes a sigh of relief
for now we know
in our deepest dreams
you were the only
one for me.

Simple

Ours is a simple story about
      complex people
finding a way to weave a silent love,
a humble love,
one that was never heard
but witnessed by
a hundred thousand souls,
maybe more!
And we want it to be
remembered
because
in its memory we find
ourselves intertwined;
the softness of your touch,
your cheek upon mine,
that fearlessness I have
grown to crave
and the way your caress
can conquer any
disconnection.
All these I ponder
with gratefulness
that I am woven
into the story
of us.

Blood Alley

What was it about the way
the wind blew right through
the dead ends at midnight,
trying to convince me
I could walk through walls
and find a new way to live,
a new way to think,
start over
in a place where there were
no blood alleys,
one-way streets and
overlord turncoats and
juggernaut jokers,
holding my soul in a case
chained to their bony wrists.
But I listened to the wind,
for once in my life
I listened to him
telling me there was more
to life than a striving for it.
And to my surprise,
it was right there
and all I had to do was
give it up
and just live it up.

Blessings

There is much
that frightens me,
much more than
what goes *bump* in the night
or at least,
this is what I tell myself.
While I can wrap myself up
in a blanket of worry,
knit for one,
and rock myself to a
restless sleep,
I will choose instead to bury
myself in an early grave
of bedsheets
and blessings.

Unwanted Guests

I think it's common to hope
that as I grove
my demons will get bored
and pack their things,
go look for some new poor soul
to bash heads with.
The reality is though,
they are a patient lot
and have become very good
at hiding in the nook of my will
and of my confidence.
So, I believe it is important for me
to always be ready to
show them the door and
fight them if I have to,
because the key to my life
is to live life
with a mind that is as
sharp as my sword.

Need vs. Want

She doesn't need me often,
so when she does call
my name,
nothing on this earth
or in Hell beneath,
will stop me from
being at her side.

Pep Talk

As you were,
Little Heart,
for this battle is
too great for your
lovely beat to comprehend.
Stay pure.
Stay innocent
as much as you can,
at least until
this war
comes to your
front door.

Spectre

Let's lose our skin,
deal out our bones
between the hellhounds
and the angels,
leave this world
so we can make
love as
spectres only can.

Baptism

Hypnotize me with the
promise of baptizing me
with all you have to offer;
spare me no luxury.
I want to work for it,
be put to the test
and run into the ground
because if I don't come away
scarred and scathed
then what was it all
good for,
to have loved you
with complete abandon?

Dew

Do not wait for him.
Do not pine for me,
but rather for the morning dew
on the day
when you have woken
and do not feel
this emptiness any longer.

Urgent Love

This is not a test;
do not adjust your life.
If you are receiving this
know that you are not alone.
this is not a test.
Love each other
like it's an
emergency.

Mirage

The feeling of contentment
today
feels like a mirage
dancing and whispering truths
I know can quench
my thirst to finally
accept the fact
that I am a broken man.
I am a broken man
who drank too much,
worried too much,
schemed too much,
lied too much,
hated too much,
and yet,
even though the mirage
promises me that
all this will go away
if I can reach it,
I am certain
I will never die of thirst
because
I think I'm going to be alright.

Lip-Sync Love

You are like my
favorite song,
pumping hard in my heart,
lips dictating the lyrics,
silently screaming
all the things
we would like to do
behind the curtain call
and in the city squares,
without a care
for who hears us.

Intentional
Confessional

I have a confession.
Before I kissed you
I skipped ahead to the end
to see what happens to us,
and though I feel guilty
for not saving anyone
who died along the way,
or saying anything about
knowing how things end,
I am glad
I never stopped reading the
lines in your face
for the always fell into place
with my
best intentions
for your heart.

Jigsaw Puzzles

When there is nothing left for you
but this feeling that the world
doesn't belong to you anymore,
and you don't think you belong to it,
it might mean that
your version of the truth
has stopped working for you.
I want to let you know,
before you try on that coat of
desperation,
that absolute truth still exists.
It is here.
For everyone.
It isn't scary.
It isn't even a burden.
It won't judge you.
It is accepting,
because the *truth* believes in
second chances
and it will show you love
that will stretch over a
multitude of disasters.
That feeling you felt
when this poem began
will be replaced
with the one you had
when you were a child
and completed your very
first puzzle.

Damnation

Will this kill us,
or will it make us stronger?
I don't know the answer
to these kinds of questions
because the answer seems
too large for me.
I keep losing myself
when trying to look too deep
and see where you and I
end up.
Too many questions
left unanswered breed
fear and loathing in me,
and have me asking more questions,
like:
Am I too old?
Do I have too many addictions?
Am I too dramatic?
But what I am certain of is that
I need your salvation
and I'm tired of
damnation.

Lessons

All this time
I was trying to get
to somewhere,
this magical destination
which old men call,
"becoming a man"
without making mistakes
and learning those lessons
your parents tried to teach you,
but you loved them
for having tried.
And while,
I'm still on this journey,
I don't have a destination
per se,
and that's okay with me.

Not knowing where you're going
makes living your life
a little more difficult
but easy is where
sheep go to die
and wolves become
alive.

Speed of Light

The stars died out
millions of years ago,
and yet their light
is ever with us.
So shall it be
with the memory
of our
first kiss.

Homecoming

Home was like a
double-edged sword,
it did me damage when I left,
and when I came back.
But,
I figure,
if I walk in the door,
bleeding but alive,
happy but sober,
know that it was worth it
because I did
it all for you.

Closer

I want to be closer,
closer to the light
that fills the space
between my body
and my spirit
because I believe
that is where
I can build
myself
a home.

Safe House

When you feel
there is nowhere
left to turn,
go straight to your heart;
there is always
a room for you there.
And the best part is,
you can stay there
for as long as you like.

Clean a Dirty Mirror

Do not kiss me with your love,
rather,
kiss me with all the fear, anger,
and any other emotion you
believe makes you
attractive.
Because when you and I
find a way
to embrace
in those moments,
the rest of our life together
will be a little bit
easier.

Dilation

While some pupils
never dilate enough
to let the light in,
live your life with
eyes wide open
and you'll brave
any darkness
you see.

Bitter

The coffee I brewed for myself
is bitter,
and it burns my tongue and throat
reminding me that there are
many things in this life
we make for ourselves
in hopes they will bring us
contentment.
Instead we often give
ourselves bitter memories
and burnt heart.
I have learned though,
all I need to do
is let it sit there
for a while
until I am ready
to try again.

Floating

When you placed
your mouth
upon mine
you breathed
hope
into my lungs
much like
helium love
for the
ballooning heart.

Little Dragons

We were little dragons
breathing our hot breath
over each other,
setting fires
in our hearts.

Forest Fires

It is okay to tremble.
There is nothing wrong
with admitting you are weak.
I have found that in
moments of self-doubt
I have to remind myself
there is a fire
burning
down
deep,
somewhere I can't feel its warmth
until I open the furnace doors
and kick up the ash
of my worry,
exposing all of the
darkness to the oxygen
and have my
Higher Power
blow gently
on that flame
and nurse me back
into a raging
forest fire.

Runaway Blake

Together,
we shorn those sheep
and dyed the wool
in tiger's blood,
made ourselves
new clothes
and wore them in the
streets of London,
looking for that place
with the dancefloor
on the second story
made out of glass.
I emptied myself
behind a couch.
You never saw
and ordered me
another.
Those clothes were
still dripping
as we left traces
of ourselves
throughout that
forsaken place.

Remote Control

It isn't easy to admit when
you are wrong,
to another,
to yourself even.
When you do
your big bad world
gets infinitely larger,
and when this happens
it is your calling to
fill it up with
the people,
places and
things
you love.

Remember,
you cannot control them,
they don't control you,
you are not a
remote control.

Knifey Spoony

The mountain air was
cold
like a knife,
and it cut our
love into portions,
each one
just large enough
to share
with each thing
we loved about
the world.

Pauper Prince

There was nothing left
and then you told me,
there was nothing left
to do
but love me.
Me,
the richest poor man
this world
had ever seen.

Pine

I am tired
of sitting on
hard benches,
pining for the
days when the
only things
we wanted to
cut were the
strings attached
to our limbs,
before they cut
down the trees
we loved to climb
in summer.
But now I see
life in dead things,
and I am no longer
afraid to live.

Gold Rush

Strength.
It is here,
in the river of your heart,
hiding beneath the stones
and the sand that life has
puts there to hide it.
So pick up your courage,
pan for that gold
and stake your claim
on a life
rich in love.

Something's Different about You

People say I look
different now,
say there is something
in my face
they have never
noticed before.
It's called
acceptance.
This is who I am,
and I am
right where
I'm supposed to be.

About the Poet

Jon Lupin is a writer, husband, and father. He shares his stories of love, healing, and restoration the best way he knows how: with poetry. Jon lives in the suburbs of Vancouver, Canada, with his wife, Rose, his three children, and his dog. You can find him on his popular Instagram account @The_PoetryBandit.